Punned Haiku

Crosbie's Book of
Punned Haiku

by John S. Crosbie

Illustrations by Roslyn Schwartz

Workman Publishing, New York

Library of Congress Cataloging in Publication Data
Crosbie, John S 1920-
Crosbie's Book of punned haiku.
1. Haiku, Canadian. 2. Humorous poetry, Canadian.
I. Title. II. Title: Book of punned haiku.
PR9199.3.C689B6   1979   811'.5'4   79-64788
ISBN 0-89480-110-4

Cover and Book Design by Charles Kreloff

Workman Publishing Company, Inc.
1 West 39 Street
New York, New York 10018

Manufactured in the United States of America

First Printing August 1979

10 9 8 7 6 5 4 3 2 1

It was while preparing the Third Edition of *Crosbie's Dictionary of Puns* that I first came under the spell of haiku. I found myself intrigued by those wonderful little gems of Japanese poetry. It is an interesting challenge to have to confine your thought to seventeen syllables and just three lines, where the first and third lines can have only five syllables and the middle line seven.

Hoping to add to the pleasure of the reader's journey through my dictionary, I began to express some of the entries in the haiku form. Then, one day, there came what was either a breakthrough or a breakdown in English literature: I found that with a little extra effort, quite often you could make the endings of the first and last lines rhyme.

With all deference to our Japanese friends, I believe that adding this requirement gives a better feel to the form. It also, of course, presents more of a challenge. This is especially true if, as I have done, you end each haiku with a pun. In effect, it creates a new word game.

I hope that the examples on the pages that follow will give you as much pleasure as I had in devising them!

—J.S.C.

If the spring bird cries
Before last snow melts, you're in
For a big sap rise.

In our youthful slacks
Thoughts of love made us tense. Now
Old, lotus relax.

If you cannot keep
A tune, you are headed for
The choir's discord heap.

There is nothing worse
Than poems about cute cats.
It is all perverse.

I grew like a weed
And never ever saw the
Things my Poppy seed.

———————⊙———————

When I learned to dance,
I paid for it by earning
Jokes at my expanse.

———————⊙———————

In youth, an ellipse
Was my shape of hair. Now I'm
Careful how eclipse.

I guess I'm quite dull:
The art of rowing never
Got into my scull!

Some night on the grass
If your approach is not crass
You will winsome lass.

They say love's fickle.
The truth is, like kissing hair,
It's elliptical.

Don't go it alone.
A ring on the finger is
Worth two on the phone.

Once, when in college,
I sought a sweet girl just for
Caramel knowledge.

Girls learn from Mother
That sex is just one damp thing
After another.

———————⊙———————

It is sadly true
That a pause in a wedding
Is oft over "do."

———————⊙———————

Should the groom falter,
The bride will deride and soon
The chapel altar.

Before you gamble
On walking the new girl home,
Try a preamble.

If seeking in haste
To be bedded or wedded
Just lose if you're chaste!

Geologists may
Seem picky, girls, but love's just
A stone's pro away!

The plot is just right:
New stewardess meets pilot;
It's love at first flight!

What a pear we'll be!
Lettuce marry. That's if you
Carrot all for me.

When the gods sought wine
To grace Olympian feasts
They first shook divine.

Yes, sex with a smile
Does promote health. A Ms. is
As good as a mile.

Liquor *is* quicker.
Besides, candy'll go to waist
And make her thicker!

Sad truth: Much drinking
Can turn a hot-eyed glance to
Just wishful winking.

The bald truth comes quick:
It's harder scalping skeptics
Than to heretic!

—————⊙—————

Lest you should bore 'em,
Let your listeners know that
You're really forum.

—————⊙—————

If to perdition
You feel graffiti'll lead us,
Sign a partition.

He who from truth shies
Can freeze his friendships, if he
Tells a paralyze.

His wife was quite sharp.
As a backseat driver she
Was his autoharp.

Though her face is bleared
I can still admire a girl
If she's nicely reared.

I am sure of this:
If you marry a widow,
You won't wed amiss.

In her girlish way
She led him in her tent and
Hoped the guy would stay.

I keep rueing it
When I melt cheese. Anyway,
It's fonduing it!

Reduce any way
You can. The best for the weak
Is to skip fry day.

It may seem quite mean
But mostly, cosmeticians
See just the porcine.

That native food gave
Me heartburn. I'm having a
Tropical eat-wave!

When taxes are due,
Americans tend to feel
Quite bled-white and blue!

———————⬤———————

To make tax forms true
They should read "Income Owed Us"
And "Incommode You."

———————⬤———————

The population
Popularly pops the Pill;
Alliteration.

Have pity on Marge:
Out of using her credit
She gets a big charge!

Life's chess game is cooked.
Unless you can pawn it, you'll
Keep on getting rooked.

When your team's huddle
Ends in a fuddle, don't get
Caught in the muddle.

In world sports, Japan
Scores many points but sometimes
Has its ah so ran.

I have found too late
You only grow poor hoarding
Your pieces of hate.

Pa does tend to roam.
He's plucking far petals save
The daisies at home.

Often the teacher
Who lectures with leers on love
Is a lay preacher.

Whatever you say
About pornography, sex
Is sure here to stray!

Things seem what they ain't.
When a girl pulls a swoon it's
Oft naught but a feint.

They say it is good
To live like old Robin Hood.
I know I Sherwood!

Now my fringe is frayed
And baldness shines ahead, I
Wish I'd made the grayed!

I have no regrets.
Some think wallabies strange but
They're my parapets.

Don't just jump and prance
With the music. Pose and say,
"May I have this stance?"

Each night until dawn
The stags all play. How time flies
When you're having fawn!

Pigs are prone to root.
That's why their taste so often
Is their strong suet.

The Ark had a till,
So the frog took a green back,
The duck took a bill.

Do owls on a toot
Get so carried away they
Just don't give a hoot?

"I'm not feeling well
Today," said the turtle, "But
Tomorrow I shell."

For a holy stint,
A moth of the cloth gave up
His woolens for lint.

Looking beside her,
Miss Muffet thought how tough it
Was someone'd spider.

Heard on Noah's ark:
"Sailing is fun but scrubbing
The decks is aardvark."

One of the great sins
Is that your life is ova
When it first begins.

Though she loved the male,
She made it clear to sailors
She was not for sail.

What perversity!
He went to view the stripper
Just her phantasy.

Belly dancers bold
Prove with their dancing all that
Shivers is not cold.

We all cherish praise,
But a hike in our pay is
The best kind of ways.

───────●───────

To some it seems true
That the meaning of Heaven's
A womb with a view.

───────●───────

The Africans teach
That well-timed silence hath more
Elephants than speech.

Before his check's sent,
Be sure your wife was treated
By the document.

Beware the sorrow
Of getting slim: Here today
And gaunt tomorrow!

If you must trip her,
The vaudeville banana skin
Makes a good slipper.

If on skis you roam,
Be careful: You'll be lucky
To get a toe home!

The skill of the Scotch
In the making of stew is
The ramparts they watch.

By sex change stricken,
He could no more rule the roost;
He was too chicken.

What can a wife say?
If you mention his bald spot,
There is hell toupee!

It was sad but true:
He could not be her brother
And assist her too.

To give you the gist
Of my fondest perversions
I sensualist.

Gertie got the gate
Since as a dancer she was
Always undulate.

―――――○―――――

Her nerves are her ruin.
She's so very high-strung that
· She's quite out of tune.

―――――○―――――

In her need to please,
She yearns to learn reading palms—
But fears climbing trees.

All grace defied her
When she was sober. Her charm
Lurked deep in cider.

Sex is here to stay—
A cheering thought for *Playboy*.
So hip, hip array!

———————⊙———————

Some think it is lewd
To walk about unclothed but
Others love denude.

———————⊙———————

The bare fact can hit
You hard: Once you're a nudist
You are stark with it.

As after the Fall
The sly snake consoled Adam,
"You can't venom all!"

That farmer's not rich.
In his hay-day somehow he
Never got the pitch.

———————○———————

Farming's just a ball.
To change pumpkins into squash
Simply let them fall!

———————○———————

Why do so many
Foods come packaged in plastic?
It's quite uncanny!

Stop your sad sobbin'!
What if your wallet's gone? It's
The Spring's first robin.

I love wind-up dolls—
But not the ones that wind up
At the shopping mauls!

———————⊙———————

Because of our fights
I quite dislike you some days—
But then love unites.

———————⊙———————

It is very nice
To recall I was young once.
Wish it had been twice!

Yours are bearable
But others' kids can make your
Hair quite terrible.

Is it not absurd;
An amateur can write prose?
It's a crazy word!

Punning makes no cents;
You cannot survive on bread
And utter nonsense!

When poets expire
They merely move on to the
Invisible quire.

Some scan fatally.
Have you been 'way out on a
Limerick lately?

Who made rhymed ado
About the names of others?
It was Clerihew.

Oscar Wilde, they say,
Was well known in his time as
Prematurely gay.

One more drink refused,
Queen Victoria declared,
"I am not bemused!"

Punsters of the world,
Should these not sate your hunger
Just eat your art out!

If you would sally
With show mermaids to dally,
Wait in finale.

---○---

Sailors are fickle.
Touchy, too. If I were you
I would nautical.

---○---

When tars overeat
The admiral then must land
On his too fat fleet.

If the play can't suit
Toss up some ripe thing—but don't
Let them see who fruit!

Your life may seem fine,
But some greet each day with dread.
They just rise and whine.

———————○———————

I would like to learn
To fight like the Greeks. But what
Does aggression earn?

———————○———————

Always drive intent
And remember that safety
Is no accident.

If there's a defect
In your old faith that bugs you,
Do try the insect.

In riding play safe;
The thrill of the hunt can bring
The joys of the chafe!

As months run their span,
If you can't tell the seasons
You're no whither man.

High above the clods
There lives the perfect gambler;
The Wizard of Odds.

Don't embarrass the
Waiter with "Is that a crack
Or a heresy?"

We note with sadness
Investing in communism
Is just share madness.

It's part of their ruse:
Diplomats must all watch their
Appease and accuse.

My son's so correct
He calls his mum Mater. But
He calls me collect.

D_o you need a truss?
Many people don't but the
Hippopotamus.

Finale

Literary crime
Or test of wit? We must quit
At some point in rhyme!

———————⊙———————

Farewell and adieu.
The rest is all up to you:
Rhyme some more haiku! *

———————⊙———————

*If you do and a pun is involved,
send it for inclusion in
Crosbie's Dictionary of Puns.
Write Box 5040, Toronto, Canada M5W 1N4.